The World's Best Golf Jokes

The World's Best Golf Jokes

Robert McCune

Illustrations by
Peter Townsend

ANGUS
& ROBERTSON
PUBLISHERS

ANGUS & ROBERTSON PUBLISHERS

Unit 4, Eden Park, 31 Waterloo Road,
North Ryde, NSW, Australia 2113, and
16 Golden Square, London W1R 4BN,
United Kingdom

First published in Australia
by Angus & Robertson Publishers in 1988
First published in the United Kingdom
by Angus & Robertson (UK) in 1988
First published in New Zealand
by Angus & Robertson NZ in 1988
Reprinted 1989 (twice)

Copyright © Mary Coleman 1988

National Library of Australia
Cataloguing-in-publication data.

  The world's best golf jokes

  ISBN 0 207 15462 7.

  1. English wit and humor.   2. Golf –
  Anecdotes, facetiae, satire, etc.
  I. Townsend, Peter.   II. Title.
828.0208

Typeset in 12/13pt Goudy Old Style
Printed in the United Kingdom by
BPCC Hazell Books Ltd

"Hey, George, did you hear the awful news about John?"

The two golfers were talking over a drink in the club bar.

"No what happened to him?"

"Well he had a great round on Wednesday — under seventy I heard — anyway he finished early and drove home, and found his wife in bed with another man! No questions asked... he just shot 'em both! Isn't it terrible?"

"Could have been worse," George commented.

"How?"

"If he'd finished early on Tuesday, he would have shot me!"

"What's your golf score?" the country club interviewer asked the prospective new member.

"Well, not so good," replied the golfer. "It's 69."

"Hey, that's not bad. In fact, it's very good."

"Glad you think so. I'm hoping to do even better on the next hole," the golfer confided.

With all its rites and refinements, many believe that golf has a venerable history. But this is far from true. It was an accident that led to the beginnings of the game.

Out on the gentle heather-clad hills one memorable day a Scottish shepherd took a wild swing at a sheep with his crook. He missed. His crook cut under the fortunate beast and accidentally hit a small, round pebble which was so neatly clipped it flew in a graceful arc down the slope. The shepherd followed after and gleefully lined up the pebble for a second swipe.

"Wha hey," he cried in delight, "now let's see if I can't hit some rabbits in yonder wee holey."

A colleague on an adjacent hill noticed a flurry of rabbit fur and leaving his flock, strolled over for a closer view — conveniently taking his heavy crook with him.

Of course that was the end of shepherding on that day. The game of golf was launched at 10.15 a.m., the first lie about a score was told at 11.30 a.m. and at midday, the first golf joke was heard over lunch in the pub.

"Just got a brand new set of clubs for my husband."
"Oh what a good trade!"

Roger and Charlie emerged from the clubhouse to tee off at the first, but Roger looked distracted.

"Anything the matter, mate?" Charlie asked.

"Oh, it's just that I can't stand the club pro," Roger replied. "He's just been trying to correct my stance."

"He's only trying to help your game," Charlie soothed.

"Yeah, but I was using the urinal at the time."

Man blames fate for other accidents but feels personally responsible when he makes a hole in one.

"I claim damages," shouted the angry man hopping on one foot and holding his ankle.

The player whose ball had connected with the pedestrian was apologetic.

"But didn't you hear me call 'fore'?" he asked.

"Four! Four!" stormed the victim. "I won't settle for anything less than a fiver."

The sky above was blue and cloudless. Only a light breeze ruffled the treetops outside the window. If the judge had been a lawmaker instead of a law interpreter he knew he would be making laws forbidding court sessions on such glorious days.

"Well," he mused, dragging his eyes back to the court, "I guess there's no way out. I might just as well tune back in on the case."

"And in addition to that, Your Honour," the barrister for the defence was droning, "my client claims she was beaten into insensibility by a golf club in the hand of her husband."

"How many strokes?" murmured the judge absently.

"Mildred, shut up," cried the golfer at his nagging wife. "Shut up or you'll drive me out of my mind."

"That," snapped Mildred, "that wouldn't be a drive. That would be a putt."

When the Maharajah of Merchandani was taken suddenly ill during a holiday in England he was attended by a young locum filling in for the Wimpole Street surgeon. The Maharajah's appendix was deftly removed and the patient was beaming.

"You saved my life," he said to the young man. "Whatever you want shall be yours."

"It was quite simple really," protested the young surgeon.

"But I am a rich man, I insist," said the princely patient.

"Well, I'd love a new set of matched golf clubs," the young doctor admitted.

"Consider it done," came the stately reply.

The surgeon forgot all about this grand promise until some weeks later when he received this cable:

HAVE YOUR CLUBS BUT SADLY ALL NOT
MATCHED STOP FOUR DO NOT HAVE
SWIMMING POOLS STOP

Paddy was playing golf at a very exclusive club in County Kerry for the first time, and on the sixth hole he hit a hole in one. Jubilant, he walked down to the green and, just as he was taking his ball from the cup, up popped a leprechaun.

"Sor," the leprechaun bowed politely and continued. "This is a very exclusive course which has everything, including the services of a leprechaun if you make a hole in one in the sixth hole. I will be delighted to grant you any wish your heart desires."

"Saints preserve us," said Paddy in shock. But seeing the leprechaun waiting so patiently he thought for a minute then admitted shyly that he did have a wish. "I want to have a longer penis," he confided.

"Your wish is granted, Sor," the leprechaun said and disappeared in a puff of green smoke down the hole.

So Paddy headed back to join up with his friends and as he walked he could feel his penis slowly growing.

The golf game progressed and Paddy's penis kept getting longer and longer until it came out beneath his shorts and reached down below his knees.

"Hmmmm," Paddy thought, "maybe this wasn't such a great idea after all." So he left his friends and went back to the sixth hole with a bucket of balls and began to shoot. Finally he hit a hole in one, and by the time he got down to the green, he had to hold his penis to keep it from dragging on the ground.

But he managed to take the ball from the cup and sure enough, out popped the leprechaun.

"Sor, this is a very exclusive course," said the leprechaun bowing once again, "and it has everything including the services of a leprechaun... oh it's you again. Well what will it be this time?"

"Could you make my legs longer?" pleaded Paddy.

Errol Flynn and W. C. Fields played many games of golf together resulting in many marvellous stories.

On one occasion the legendary swashbuckler and the legendary drunk were playing when Fields dislocated his knee. Flynn helped him back to the clubhouse where the professional offered to push the knee back in.

"But it will be quite painful," he warned.

"Proceed, my good man," said W. C., taking a long swig from his indispensable hip flask. "Pain means nothing to me."

The pro took a firm grip on the knee and pushed hard. Fields let out a howl of pain.

"Easy, Mr Fields," said the pro. "My wife had a baby a couple of days ago and she didn't make half that fuss."

"Yes, but they weren't trying to push it back in," retorted Fields.

"It was golf that drove me to drink," the great comedian once admitted, "and you know, I don't know how to thank it."

On another occasion Fields was asked if he believed in clubs for women.

"Yes," he answered, "if every other form of persuasion fails."

The Monte Carlo golf course is famed for its glorious position high in the hills behind the town — a place of lush beauty and tranquillity unless your game is off. Charlie's game was!

Not one of his shots went right. At the eighteenth hole he made a last swipe at the ball, missed completely, and tore up about a metre of turf.

He then strolled disgustedly from the tee and looked down to the blue Mediterranean. Sailing boats were to be seen gliding about hundreds of metres below.

"How," demanded Charlie, "how can anyone be expected to shoot a decent game with those infernal ships rushing back and forth."

"Why don't you play golf with Captain Fortescue any more, John?" the young wife enquired.

"Well, would you play golf with a man who talks when you're putting, fiddles his score and moves his ball out of the rough when you're not looking?"

"Certainly not!"

"Neither will the Captain."

A group of golfers were putting on the green when suddenly a ball dropped in their midst. One of the party winked at the others and shoved the ball into the hole with his foot.

Seconds later a very fat player puffed on to the green quite out of breath and red of face. He looked round distractedly and then asked:

"Seen my ball?"

"Yeah, it went in the hole," the joker answered with straight-faced alacrity.

The fat one looked at him unbelievingly. Then he walked to the hole, looked in, reached down and picked up his ball. His astonishment was plain to see. Then he turned, ran down the fairway and as he neared his partner the group on the green heard him shout:

"Hey, Sam, I got an eleven."

An attack of grippe laid Snavely low just before his usual weekend game. He rested for a couple of weeks and looked forward to being back on the links. But just as he was about to play again, the grippe returned.

His regular opponent was miffed and grumbled at the other end of the telephone.

"Why can't you play this time, Snavely?" he wanted to know.

"Let me put it this way," said the sufferer sadly. "My trouble is an overlapping grippe."

What do you do when your opponent claims to have found his ball in the rough and you know he's a liar because his ball is in your pocket?

"I see a Russian says he has invented a game which closely resembles golf."
"Oh yes, my husband's been playing that for years."

A golf professional, hired by a big department store to give golf lessons, was approached by two women.

"Do you wish to learn to play golf, madam?" he asked one.

"Oh, no," she replied, "it's my friend who's interested in learning. I learned last Wednesday."

"**I**'d move heaven and earth to be able to break 100 on this course," sighed the veteran.

"Try heaven," advised the caddie. "You've already moved most of the earth."

"**I** gather you make more money in a year than Ronald Reagan," a nosey stranger asked a leading professional.

"Yeah, well why not?" came the reply. "I'm a better player than he is."

"**I**f you spend so much time at golf you won't have anything laid aside for a rainy day."

"Oh won't I just! You should see my desk. It's just groaning with the work that I've put aside for a rainy day."

A visitor about to play the second dogleg at the Killarney Golf Club hit his ball into the woods. He went to retrieve it and came upon a witch stirring a large cauldron. As the steam billowed up, the man stood watching it transfixed.

"What's in there?" he asked finally.

"Ah, this is a magic brew," the witch cackled. "If you drink this, you will have the best golf game in the world! Nobody will be able to beat you!"

"I'd give anything in the world for that," said the man.

"Well you shall have it," replied the crone. "But I must warn you there's a penalty for having such power. You will not only have the best game in the world but you will have the worst sex life. Is that something you're prepared for?"

The golfer paused for a moment to consider; then, without a word, he held out his hand for a cup of the brew.

He returned to his game and immediately hit a hole in one. Soon after he became club champion, soon after that he became the best player in the country and soon after that he won every major international tournament there was.

A year later and now acknowledged as the world's best player, he was playing at the same course and he remembered his past experience. He decided to see if the witch was still there and indeed he found her still in the same place still bent over the cauldron.

"Ah, it's you," she said. "Tell me how is your game of golf?"

"The best there is," replied the man with honesty.

"Ah, and what about your sex life?" she cackled.

"Not bad," he replied.

"Eh? What's that? What do you call 'not bad'?"

"Well I had sex three, maybe four times last year."

"Three, four!" shrieked the witch, "and you call that 'not bad'!"

"As parish priest at Ballymooney, I find it not too much of a hardship."

The tall highlander walked into the shop at Pitlochry Golf Club and stood ramrod straight as he pulled a badly nicked ball from his sporran.

"What can you do?" he asked the manager.

"Well," said the manager in complete understanding, "we can vulcanise it for five pence or re-cover it for ten."

"I'll let ye know t'morra," said the customer.

The next day he was back, holding out the ball. "Tha' Regiment," he said, "votes ta' vulcanise."

"That's good for one long drive and a putt," said the cocky golfer as he teed his ball and looked down the fairway to the green. He swung mightily and hit his ball which landed about a metre from the tee. His caddie handed him a club and remarked:
"And now for one hell of a putt."

"Can ye see your way to letting me have a golf ball, Jock?" Ian asked his old friend.
"But Ian, you said you were going to stop playing golf," said Jock reluctantly handing over an old spare.
"By degrees, Jock. By degrees," replied Ian pocketing the ball. "I've stopped buying balls as a first step."

Friendly golfer (to player searching for lost ball):
"What sort of a ball was it?"
Caddie (butting in):
"A brand new one — never been properly hit yet!"

He'd been marooned on the island for almost five years and had given up hope of being saved. He had resigned himself to living alone for the rest of his days without the solace of human company.

One day, however, a beautiful woman clad only in a wetsuit swam onto the shore of his island. She was the lone survivor of another wreck.

The castaway gasped and ran to meet her. Overjoyed at having someone to talk to he blurted out his whole story — how he'd managed to live off the land, surviving by his wits and so on. It was marvellous to speak with another human being.

"Good heavens," the woman cried breaking into his narrative, "you mean you've been on this island for five years?"

"That's right," said the man.

"Tell me," she asked in a husky voice as she brushed a blonde lock of hair out of her large and lovely eyes, "did you smoke cigarettes before you were marooned?"

"Yes, yes, I did," he remembered with pleasure.

"Well, since you haven't had a cigarette for so long, here!" and the beauty unzipped a pocket in the wetsuit and produced a packet of cigarettes which she gave to him.

As she leant close to light his cigarette for him the new arrival murmured, "Were you a drinking man before you got shipwrecked?"

"Well," said the man contentedly puffing, "I did enjoy the occasional whisky."

The woman unzipped another pocket and produced a hip flask which she offered him.

He took a pull from the flask and was thanking her when she leant closer to him and whispered, "You've been here for five years and in all that time I guess you haven't, um, played around either have you?" And as she spoke she began to pull down the zip at the front of her wetsuit.

"Good heavens," he said in high excitement. "Don't tell me you have a set of clubs in there as well."

Caddying for the elderly beginner had required great patience. He was doddery but he was dogged and he had sworn to break 100 before the summer was out. In fact there was a bottle of malt riding on it — his faithful caddie would receive it when the magic score had been broken.

Then arrived a day when dogged persistence seemed about to pay off for both player and caddie. They were on the green at the eighteenth and only 97 strokes had been accounted for. Player and caddie were excited and in the grip of such emotion it was small wonder that the player sent his first putt racing three metres past the hole.

In a flash the caddie had dropped the flagstick, picked up the ball and was crying excitedly.

"Well done, sir! You've done it! You've done it! Anyone would give you that."

Having led an interestingly dissolute life composed largely of women, drinking, gambling and golf, but not necessarily in that order, at the end of it, the new arrival was not too surprised to find himself in hell. He was however quite surprised to find that his particular corner of Hades was an eighteen-hole golf course complete with gentle woods, a cooly serene lake, well kept fairways, an immaculate green and a clubhouse with the usual professional's shop. The reprobate's delight was complete when he read the shop's notice.

HELP YOURSELF. ALL EQUIPMENT FREE.

"Well, this is going to be tough to take," he leered as he chose a bag containing perfectly matched clubs. So laden he ambled to the first tee where he took out a driver, gave a delighted practice swing and then felt in the ball pocket. It was empty.

He was about to return to the shop to remedy the situation when he noticed a grinning figure in red.

"Don't mind me," the grin grew wider, "and don't bother going back for balls. There aren't any. That's the hell of it!"

Morris was a man who knew all there was to know about golf. He knew all the courses, the champions, their scores, as well as the prize money the professionals had won for the past fifty years or more. He had read every book ever published on the game and knew all there was to know about technique, but, strange to say, he had never played a game.

Having listened to him hold forth for so long his friends finally ganged up on him and insisted that he play a game. It was arranged for the following weekend.

Morris set out with borrowed clubs and faced the eighteen holes of his home course. Five hours later he returned with a score of 63 which included four eagles, nine birdies and a hole in one. Never had anyone seen such a fine performance from a beginner.

However while the celebrations were going on in the clubhouse, Morris announced that he would never play again.

"What!" cried his distraught mates. "What!" echoed the equally distraught pro. "But you could win all sorts of prizes for the club. You know everything there is to know about the game."

"Not everything," Morris replied. "The books didn't tell me I'd have to walk."

Tickets for the British Open are hard to get and the touts have a field day. One keen spectator was offered a ticket for £50.

"That's absurd," the enthusiast declared. "Why, I could get a woman for that!"

"True sir, but with this ticket you get eighteen holes!"

Mulholland believed himself a superior caddie. He certainly had a superior attitude towards the man whose clubs he carried. Why only last month he had caddied for Lee Trevino, and now each time his client asked for a 5−wood, the boy would sneer, "Lee Trevino used a 4−iron from here."

And so it continued all the way around. The caddie recommended the clubs Trevino would have used and the golfer's game went rapidly from bad to worse.

Finally, at the eighteenth, there was a huge lake to cross.

"OK, know-all," said the golfer, "what would Trevino suggest here?"

"I think if Lee had come this far with you, he'd say, 'Use an old ball.'"

"When can you let me have another session?" a golfer asked his professional who was a veteran of 75 years.

"Tomorrow morning," came the reply, "but not tomorrow afternoon. That's when I visit my father."

"Goodness me," exclaimed the student incredulously, "how old is he then?"

"He's 95."

"And he's a good player too?"

"Ah no sir — he knocks the ball about a bit — but, bless him, he'll never make a player."

"My wife says that if I don't give up golf she'll leave me."

"Say, that's tough, old man."

"Yeah, I'm going to miss her."

"Now," said the golf pro, "suppose you just go through the motions without driving the ball."

"But that's precisely the difficulty I'm trying to overcome," said his pupil.

He'd sliced his drive and watched resignedly as the ball plummeted into the woods. He followed after and found his ball — surrounded by thick undergrowth and wedged firmly between two tree roots.

He contemplated the situation for a few profoundly silent minutes then turned to his caddie and asked:

"You know what shot I'm going to take here?"

"Yes, sir," replied the boy as he took a hip flask of malt from the bag.

"Caddiemaster, that boy isn't even eight years old."

"Better that way, sir. He probably can't count past ten."

It takes real commitment to play on the Royal Nairobi course. It is bounded on three sides by a wildlife reserve the wildlife of which do not necessarily feel hesitant about grazing on greens or golfers, according to palate preferences.

The young Mormon missionary had great faith — even as he sliced his tee shot into a pretty rugged area off the course. He knew he'd find his ball and he did — between the forelegs of a huge and hungry lion.

As he fell quivering to his knees before the great beast the young man began to pray and to his astonishment the lion knelt also.

"Glory be to God," exclaimed the young evangelist, "a practising Christian lion."

"Rowrrl," roared the lion, "quiet while I'm saying grace!"

Time for a quick moral observation, the parson thought as he watched his partner's ball fly into a devilishly tricky sand trap on the fourth.

"I have observed," he said, "that the best golfers are not addicted to bad language."

His partner swept a load of sand into space and, looking down at his ball still nestling between his feet, said:

"What in the bloody hell have they got to swear about?"

The new wife was trying to fathom the mysteries of the game that so occupied her spouse's time.

"What is a handicapped golfer?" she asked.

"One who plays with his boss," came the reply.

Rich Texans are fabled for their grand style but when one oil tycoon appeared at a local British golf course followed by a servant pulling a foam-cushioned chaise-longue, his opponents thought that this was taking style too far.

"J. R., are you going to make that poor caddie lug that couch all over the course after you?" he was asked.

"Caddie, my eye," explained J. R. "That's my psychiatrist."

Isn't it great to get out on the old golf course again and lie in the sun?

W omen are cunning golfers: they shout "fore", hit 7, and score 3.

T wo golfers, slicing their drives into the rough, went in search of the balls. They searched for a long time without success while a dear old lady watched them with a kind and sympathetic expression.

At last, after the search had proceeded for half an hour, she addressed them sweetly.

"I hope I'm not interrupting, gentlemen," she said, "but would it be cheating if I told you where they are?"

N othing counts in a golf game like your opponent.

There was a bit of a queue beginning to form up at the Pearly Gates. "Something of a delay up front" was the word that went back to those waiting admission. St Peter was giving some new arrival a bit of the third degree.

"Yers," said that most venerable saint, "well despite what could be classified as an exemplary life, we do have record here of an occasion when you took the name of the Lord in vain. That'll need some explaining."

"Ah yes, I remember it well," said the mild-mannered applicant. "Pebble Beach Golf Course, 1962."

"Pebble Beach, eh?" said the saintly gatekeeper looking up with a start of interest from his records. "Difficult course, that."

"Yes indeed, sir. And that day I was on the last hole and only needed a par four to break 70 for the first time in my life."

"How was your drive?" St Peter asked sitting forward.

"Great, right down the centre of the fairway. But when I got to my ball it had fallen behind an empty Coke tin embedded in the turf."

"Oh dear," said St Peter. "Tight spot eh? Is that when you..."

"No, I'm OK with my irons. I managed to clip it neatly and it made the green but the wind caught it and rolled it off the lip and into a bunker."

"Ah," said St Peter. "Always was a windy course that. So that's when you..."

"No, no. It was still worth a try so I just dug in and

swung. The ball, plus a great quantity of sand landed on the green and the ball rolled to within 20 centimetres of the hole."

"JESUS CHRIST!" shrieked St Peter. "Don't tell me you missed the goddam putt!"

Meanwhile down below...
The Reverend Dolan was beginning to regret accepting the invitation to play golf with two members of his congregation. They had also asked the local golf pro to join them and, although the minister's handicap was respectable, his game was sadly lacking that afternoon. The pro was far from sympathetic and at every less than perfect stroke, sneered at what he called the minister's ungodly game.

He was still sneering back in the clubhouse and loud-mouthing the minister's mistakes for all to hear, when he delivered his final shot as the minister downed his ale and made to leave.

"Let's do it again, Reverend. If you can find anybody else to make it a foursome, I'd be glad to play you again."

"We might have a game next Saturday," replied the man of the cloth. "I doubt if any of my friends can play, but why don't you invite your parents and after the game I could marry them for you."

Greg Norman, in need of a well-earned rest, flew his family off to Nepal. But like any golfer on holiday, he had of course to try the local links — a mountainous course situated high in the Himalayas.

The club was delighted to welcome him but desolated that they couldn't provide a caddie as the Sherpas who usually attended were on an Everest expedition. However, they assured him they could provide a yak who would serve very well instead.

"Sahib Norman," assured the secretary, "this animal is of inestimable value but you have to watch out for him as he does like to sit on golf balls. It is, however, no problem as you have merely to reach under him and remove the ball. The yak will then continue on with the caddying."

Forewarned and only slightly perturbed, Greg set out. Over the first eight holes he had only had to remove the ball from beneath the sitting yak twice. Then on the ninth hole he had to drive the ball blind over a rocky outcrop. The yak took off after it and Greg followed the yak. He caught up with it beyond the rocks. It was sitting in a water hazard — right up to its neck.

Greg stripped off and dived in the icy water to rescue his ball. He groped around under the yak but could not feel it at all. He surfaced, took another deep breath and tried again. Still nothing. Almost frozen, he tried again but with the same result.

Finally he gave up and frozen to the bone made his way back to the clubhouse.

"Hey fella, what's going on?"

He explained to the secretary how he had dived three times for his ball but that the yak refused to move. He told the man how he couldn't find his ball and was

almost frozen to death in the process. "And," he went on, "that bloody yak is still sitting out there in the water hazard."

"Oh, a thousand pardons, Sahib." The secretary was very apologetic. "I forgot to tell you. That yak also likes to sit on fish."

"Hang it all, Harry, you can't expect me to pay that!" The two golfers were discussing a bill that Harry the hospital administrator had sent to Bill, a recent father for the first time.

"I mean Harry, £25 for the use of the delivery room. It's just not on, old man. You know I didn't get the wife there in time and the baby was born on the hospital's front lawn."

Harry leant over, took the bill, crossed out the offending entry and substituted another.

"Greens Fee £25," it read.

Which brings to mind MacDonald.

MacDonald was aged 80 when, for the first time in his life, he walked into his golf club bar and ordered drinks for everyone.

"What's the occasion, mon?" enquired the stunned bartender. "Hole in one?"

"No," the old highlander replied, "I've just married a bonnie lass!"

It was seven months later when MacDonald again strode into the bar and again ordered drinks all round.

"And what are we celebrating this time?" asked the amazed bartender.

" 'Tis the wife, lad, she's just presented me with a baby boy."

"But you've only been married seven months!"

" 'Tis true, 'tis true! Imagine it — two under par and me with a whippy shaft!"

"What's the matter?" Charlie asked impatiently.

Charlie and Jim were teeing off but Jim was rather a long time taking his stance.

"My wife came along with me today — she's watching me now from the clubhouse, and I want to make this next shot a good one," Jim explained.

"Good lord," Charlie exploded, "you haven't got a hope of hitting her at this distance."

He'd rejected the idea of dieting, health spas and swimming but when his doctor advised golf, the corpulent patient thought it might be worth trying. After a few weeks, however, he was back at the doctor's and asking whether he could take up some other game.

"But," protested the doctor, "what's wrong with golf? There's no finer game!"

"You are doubtless correct," the patient replied, "but my trouble is that when I put the wretched ball where I can see it I can't hit it and when I put it where I can hit it, I can't see it!"

"Honestly, I took twelve hours to play my round," a husband was explaining to his furious wife.

"What! For eighteen holes?" his wife asked in obvious disbelief.

"Well sixteen, actually. Browning died of a heart attack on the second and it's such slow going when you have to hit the ball, drag a body, hit the ball, drag a body, hit..."

"How many strokes d'ye have, laddie?" the Scot asked his guest after the first hole.

"Seven."

"I took six. Ma' hole."

They played the second hole and once again the Scot asked: "How many strokes?"

"Oh no sir!" said the guest. "It's my turn to ask."

Three visitors to the Royal Eastborne Club decided to join forces for a game but, of course, they first introduced themselves to each other.

"My name is Avram Solomon," said the bearded gent, "but I'm not the Rabbi."

"My name is Attila, but I'm not the Hun," said the quietly spoken youth wearing glasses.

"My n-n-n-name is M-M-M-Mary," said the shy young woman, "and I'm not a v-v-v-v-v-very good player."

It might have been Arnie Palmer or then again it could have been Gary Player — anyhow it was one of the famous professionals...

He hit his drive deep into the woods for the third time that day.

"The number four axe I think," he said with aplomb while turning to his caddie.

Saturday night and the clubhouse was crowded and noisy. The two players were drinking at the bar and discussing their game.

"Excuse me," the barman interrupted, "you're new members, aren't you?"

"Yes," replied one player, "but in all this crowd, how did you know?"

"You put your drinks down."

It was a heavenly day, enough to tempt the saints themselves from celestial chores and onto the links. And there was Jesus out on the course playing a few holes with St Michael as his caddie. As Jesus was about to make a drive He turned to St Michael and asked, "Which club do you think I should use for this shot?"

St Michael looked carefully over the course. "The 7–iron," he said.

"I don't know," said Jesus. "I think Jack Nicklaus would use the nine."

St Michael shook his head. "I think you'd better use the 7–iron, Jesus. Look, you have the sand trap in front of the green, and the lake beyond."

"Nah," said Jesus. "I think Jack Nicklaus would use the nine. Give me the nine."

So St Michael handed Jesus the 9–iron, and Jesus hit the ball. It went sailing out, bounced once on the green and then fell into the lake.

So they followed it down to the lake and, of course, Jesus walked across the water to find his ball.

A newcomer to heaven happened to pass by, saw Jesus walking on the water and asked St Michael, "Who does that guy think he is, Jesus Christ?"

"Naaah," said St Michael. "He thinks he's Jack Nicklaus."

Another day and the heavenly pair are at it again. While St Michael leant on his clubs, Jesus teed off. It was an awful shot. It screamed off the tee and disappeared deep in the rough. Then, suddenly a rabbit darted out onto the fairway with the ball in its mouth. Seconds later an eagle swooped down and carried the rabbit over the green. The rabbit squealed in terror and dropped the ball right into the cup. Hole in one.

St Michael turned to Jesus and said: "Look mate, there's money on this game. Now you gonna play or fool around?"

The secretary could see there might be trouble. The club's most straight-laced member was drawn against the bloke from Wagga whose language was so rich it would curl the tail feathers of a dead galah. The secretary took the Wagga wordsmith aside and pointed out to him how his language might give offence and begged him to try to modify it during the game.

All went well for several holes until, at the fifth dog-leg the bloke from Wagga hit his ball with a resounding whack right into the middle of the mulga.

It was too much for him and a string of colourful expletives reverberated over the course.

But quickly afterward he remembered himself and strode across the fairway to his opponent.

"I do beg your pardon," he said. "I bloody meant to say bugger."

Then there was the caddie with a similarly embarrassing vocabulary and reputation. He'd been assigned to caddie for the local Anglican bishop and warned by the caddiemaster to say nothing unless spoken to.

Things went well for a couple of holes. Then on the third the bishop's stroke was not quite clean.

"Where did that sod go, caddie?" asked the churchman looking to replace a divot he'd shifted.

"Into the bloody bunker," retorted the caddie who'd watched the ball, "and don't forget you started it."

"You think so much of your old golf game that you don't even remember when we were married."

"Of course I do, my dear. It was the day I sank that nine-metre putt."

Max had to admit it. There were many good things to be said about having a wife who was also a golfer. For one thing such wives understood and, for another, sometimes they could play a game together — as witness today.

They were teeing off from the eleventh when his drive veered from the course and came to rest behind the garage of a house built near the links.

It was his wife who pointed out that in fact the garage was directly between his ball and the links and that, rather than take a penalty he could try hitting it low with a 3-iron through the open garage doors and out the window on the opposite wall. Great idea.

Unfortunately his swing was a bit cramped and caught his beloved right between the eyes, felling her mortally in the instant.

About a year later he was playing the very same hole, this time accompanied by a caddie. Once again he sliced the ball and it fell almost in the same place.

The caddie pointed out that if he used a 3-iron and played a low shot through the open garage door and window opposite, there'd be no need to take the penalty shot.

"Oh no," replied Max, "not again. Last time I did that I wound up with a triple bogey!"

And speaking of games...
There was this Englishman and this Scotsman who were preparing to shoot a round of golf on the Royal and Ancient Golf Club of St Andrews. The Sassenach, a bow-legged squire from the Dales, stood near the tee while the Scot made a few practice swings. Then the bow legs proved too much for the Scot and obeying a mischievous urge, he sent the ball whistling between them.

"I say, old chap," the Englishman's tone was indignant, "that isn't cricket."

"No 'tis not," grinned the highlander, "it's good croquet, thought."

"I want you to know that this is not the game I usually play," snapped an irate golfer to his caddie.

"I should hope not, sir. But tell me," enquired the caddie, "what game *do* you usually play?"

On the seventeenth of the Wentworth Club Course a very careful player was studying the green. First he got down on his hands and knees to check out the turf between his ball and the hole. Then he flicked several pieces of grass out of the way and getting up he held up a wet finger to try out the direction of the wind. Then turning to his caddie he asked:

"Was the green mowed this morning?"

"Yes, sir."

"Right to left or left to right?"

"Right to left, sir."

The golfer putted . . . and missed the hole completely. He whirled on the caddie, "What TIME?"

"Well what do you think of my game?" the enthusiastic golfer asked his friend.

"It's OK, I guess," replied the friend, "but I still prefer golf."

The club secretary was apologetic. "I'm sorry, sir, but we have no time open on the course today."

"Now just a minute," the member rejoined. "What if I told you Mr Denis Thatcher and partner wanted a game. Could you find a starting time for them?"

"Yes, of course I would."

"Well, I happen to know that he's in Scotland at the moment, so we'll take his time."

After a three-month golfing tour in America the professional was at home in bed with his wife making up for his absence. Their romantic reunion was suddenly interrupted by a loud knocking at the door.

"Great heavens, that must be your husband!" cried the golfer, jumping out of bed and fumbling for his trousers.

"No, no. It can't be," replied the wife. "He's in America playing golf."

"You surely don't want me to hole that?" the pompous amateur blustered. His ball was about thirty centimetres from the hole but his opponent, a professional, answered quietly.

"No."

The amateur picked up his ball and walked on to the next tee. He was about to take the honour when he was interrupted by his opponent.

"My honour, I think," said the professional. "I won the last hole, as you didn't putt out."

"But you said you didn't want me to hole out," spluttered the amateur.

"That's right. I didn't. And you didn't."

"Good lord, Binky," the old admiral roared to his friend as he came into the clubhouse looking anything but pleased. "I've just been playing with a chappie from the Treasury. One of those civil service wallahs."

"Good oh, Bunny," replied the other old regular absently. "Bring him in for a drink."

"Can't," replied the old sea dog. "Playing the sixteenth someone shouted 'fore' and the blighter sat down to wait for a cup of tea. I've come in and left him sitting there."

Happily innocent of all golfing lore, Sam watched with interest the efforts of the man in the bunker to play his ball.

At last it rose amid a cloud of sand, hovered in the air and then dropped on the green and rolled into the hole.

"Oh my stars," Sam chuckled, "he'll have a tough time getting out of that one."

Same infuriating bunker, different infuriating spectator.

To Bill's wife, golf was a total mystery. She never could understand why Bill insisted on tiring himself by walking so far every time he played.

One day she went with him to see for herself what the game was about. For six holes she tramped after him. It was on the seventh that he landed in the infamous bunker where he floundered about for some time in the sand.

She sat herself down composedly and, as the sand began to fly she happily ventured:

"There, I knew you could just as well play in one place if you made up your mind to!"

He was a smooth operator, and at the club's annual dance he attached himself to the prettiest girl in the room and was boasting to her.

"You know, Jill, they're all afraid to play me. What do you think my handicap is?"

"I'd say your bad breath," came the quick response.

A little liquid refreshment at the nineteenth is of course all part of the game but the two Scots enthusiasts had partaken of nothing else but the national beverage throughout a long lunch break.

They returned to the links and played five holes before collecting themselves and their thoughts together.

"How do we stand, mon?" Jock asked.

"I dinna ken, Jock," Sandy spoke very carefully. "I'd say it was just a miracle."

It was a masterly addressing of the ball, a magnificent swing — but, somehow, a muddled slice shot resulted. The major's ball hit a man at full force and down he went.

The major and his partner ran up to the stricken victim who lay sprawled on the fairway. He was quite unconscious and between his legs lay the offending missile.

"Good heavens," cried the major with considerable alarm. "What shall I do?"

"We ought not to move him," said his partner, "so he becomes an immovable obstruction, and you can either play the ball as it lies or drop it two club-lengths away."

"If I died, would you remarry?" asked the wife.
"Probably would," came the reply.
"And would you let her be your golfing partner?"
"Yes, I think so."
"But surely you wouldn't give her my clubs?"
"Oh no. She's left-handed."

He was rolling in it. Made his money in scrap metal after the war and on retirement he had almost everything he wanted including time to enjoy himself — even time to take up golf.

He bought the best of everything he needed. Great clubs, shoes, sweaters as worn by the professionals, the lot, and he attacked his first game with gusto.

Behind him he left fairways looking like they'd been ploughed and greens looking like moles had surfaced in their hundreds. There were broken flag pins, clubs and mangled balls left in his wake, along with beercans, fag butts and a littering of discarded score cards.

His score was 285 which he celebrated over a steak and a pint.

"Excuse me, sir," a discreet voice interrupted his mastications. "I'm the convenor of the Greens Committee."

The novice looked around, his face filled with indignation.

"You're just the bloke I want to see. These brussels sprouts are cold!"

Then there was the New Zealander holidaying in Ireland and trying out Limerick's public course, famed for its difficulty.

Driving from thick woods on the twelfth, he aimed for the fairway but as he could not see it yelled "Fore!" and swiped. His ball struck a local player.

"Arrah, ye great mullock," cried the Irishman, as the Kiwi emerged in pursuit of his ball.

"But I called, 'Fore' and that's the signal to get out of the way."

"Well, when oi call, 'Foive,' that's the signal to punch your jaw! Foive!"

Overheard in the clubhouse bar:
        "Giving up golf, Andy! Have you lost interest then?"

"Na, na. Lost ma ball."

"Why so sad?"
    "Doctor says I can't play golf."
    "He's played with you, too?"

"Did you hear about old Wilkins collapsing at the thirteenth hole?"

"Yes, Herbert gave him the kiss of life and was drunk for seven hours."

"That can't be my ball, caddie. It looks far too old."

"It's a long time since we started, sir."

Father Patrick, who was not averse to berating his congregation for abusing the Sabbath, still liked to sneak off occasionally for a quick round of the course before the early morning service. At crack of dawn one midsummer morning he was spotted on the tenth tee one Sunday by an angel; and the angel was much annoyed.

"Father, he should be punished!" he said as he reported the miscreant to God.

"And so he shall be, my son. Watch this!" the heavenly Father replied.

Father Patrick hit off on the 590-metre, par five hole, and his ball arced gracefully in direct line with the pin. It dropped onto the green and a gentle breeze caught it and carried it a few centimetres right into the hole.

The angel turned a puzzled face to God. "Sir, I thought you were going to punish him and instead you've given him what every golfer dreams of — a hole in one and on the longest hole on the course!"

The good Lord smiled. "I *have* punished him! Who can he tell?"

"I'm going to have to give up golf," Mick sadly advised the club secretary. "I've become so nearsighted I keep losing balls and if I play with glasses they keep falling off."

"Listen, don't give up;" the secretary replied. "What about teaming up with old Bob Sullivan."

"But he's in his 80s and can only just make it around the course."

"Yes, yes, he's old, but he's also farsighted and he'll be able to see where you've hit your ball. It's a way to stay on playing."

The next day Mick and old Bob played their first game together. Mick teed off first and his powerful swing took the ball sailing up the fairway.

"Did you see it?" he asked Bob.

"Yes," the old-timer answered.

"Where did it go?"

"I forget!" came the reply.

A noted doctor's wife asked him why he never would let her play golf with him.

"My dear," he replied, "there are three things a man must do alone: testify, die and putt."

As he was walking his dog one weekday afternoon, J. P. Doneover, the bookie the punters loved to hate, espied a young lad upon the local links. J. P. stopped for a moment to watch him tee off and stayed for longer when he saw that the boy had talent. Indeed he had holed his tee shot.

He was about to call out his congratulations when the lad teed up again and once more holed in one.

Now J. P., never one to let an opportunity pass, walked up to the youngster, congratulated him and asked:

"How old are you, sonnie?"

"Eleven, sir," the young person replied.

"Anyone else here seen you play?" J. P. enquired.

Having received the assurance that no one had, J. P. proposed a match the very next day with the club champion lined up against the young tyro. The odds were handsome — 10 to 1 against the new young player.

The lad, however, took 11 at the first hole and went on around the course in much the same way. Of course he lost badly.

J. P. was furious. "You've made me look a right Charlie my lad. What's the idea of pretending you can't play?"

"Listen, dope," the youngster whispered, "next week you'll get 100 to 1."

"I'll go and ask if we can go through," said Max to Jerry.

The two golfers had been concerned for some time at the snail-like progress of two women, originally some holes ahead and now just in front of them on the ninth fairway.

Max returned after only a few paces towards the ladies.

"Jerry, this is very embarrassing, but would *you* mind going. That's my wife up ahead and she's playing with my mistress."

Jerry returned having got no further forward than Max.

"I say," he said, "what a coincidence."

"These are terrible links, caddie. Absolutely terrible."

"Sorry, sir, these ain't the links — we left them about forty minutes ago."

He'd been playing for twenty years and he'd never managed it — the ultimate goal, a hole in one.

As he was chipping away in a sandtrap one day and moving nothing but sand, he voiced the thought.

"I'd give anything," he said, "*anything* to get a hole in one."

"Anything?" came a voice from behind and he turned to see a grinning, red-clad figure with neatly polished horns and sharpened tail.

"What did you have in mind?" the golfer enquired.

"Well would you give up half your sex life?"

"Yes, yes I would."

"It's a deal then," and the figure faded discreetly from sight.

On the very next hole he did it. The ball just soared from his club in a perfect arc right into the hole. And for good measure, every other hole he played that round he holed in one.

As he was putting his clubs away the figure in red appeared once more.

"Now for our bargain," he said. "You remember you must give up half your sex life."

The golfer frowned. "That gives me a bit of a problem," he said.

"You're not backing out of this," cried the figure with a swish of its tail. "We'd struck a bargain and you agreed to it."

"Yes, of course. But I do have a problem. Which half of my sex life do you want — the thinking or the dreaming?"

Overheard on the links:
"Your trouble is that you're not addressing the ball correctly."
"Yeah, well I've been polite to the bloody thing for long enough."

That summer was a particularly hot one, but the Englishman who was on a golfing tour of the Continent gloried in the heat even though in Italy it had most of the locals gasping.

He was playing towards the fourth hole at Pisa's Golf and Country Club when he came across a player who was completely naked and cooling herself in the water hazard.

Being a discreet soul, he cleared his throat to let her know he was there. She took no notice.

"Er, I say, hello," he called hesitantly in case she hadn't heard his previous approach. "Er, I believe I've taken you unawares."

"Well," came a languid reply, "you justa' putta' 'em back!"

And talk about hazards...

At New Zealand's Rotorua Club they include bubbling mud pools, quicksand and steaming geysers and the water hazards are hot and fast flowing.

A visiting American player on the twelfth came across a quicksand bog. Extending from it was a hand gesticulating wildly.

"My, oh my," said the Yank, "is he signalling for his wedge?"

A golfing clergyman had been beaten badly by a parishioner some thirty years his senior. He returned to the clubhouse, disappointed and a trifle depressed.

"Cheer up," said his opponent. "Remember, you win at the finish. You'll probably be burying me someday."

"Yes, but even then," said the cleric, "it will be your hole."

The schoolteacher was taking her first golf lesson. "Is the word spelled 'put' or 'putt'?" she asked the instructor.

"'Putt' is correct," he replied. "'Put' means to place a thing where you want it. 'Putt' means merely a vain attempt to do the same thing."

"You have got to be the worst caddie in the world!"

"Impossible, sir. That would be too much of a coincidence."

"You're late teeing off, Bill."

"Yeah, well it being Sunday I had to toss a coin to see whether I should go to church or come to golf."

"But why *so* late?"

"Well, I had to toss twelve times."

Frank joined a threesome; and as he'd had a very successful day he was invited back the next day for a game at 8 a.m.

"Look fellers, I'd sure like to play," said Frank, "but I could be two minutes late!"

Next morning he showed up right on time, played another lovely round but this time he played every stroke left-handed.

Again, he was invited to join the threesome at 8 a.m. the following day.

"Sure, I'll be here," said Frank, "but remember I could be late, but it will only be a couple of minutes!"

"We'll wait," one of the golfers assured him. "But by the way, could you explain something that's been mystifying us all. Yesterday you played right-handed and today you played left-handed. Obviously you're proficient at both so how do you decided which way to play?"

"Ah well," Frank answered, "when I wake up in the morning, if my wife's lying on her right side, I play right-handed and if she's lying on her left side, I play left-handed. Simple as that."

"But what if she's lying on her back?"

"That's when I'm two minutes late!"

By the time a man can afford to lose a golf ball, he can't hit that far.

The four friends were out enjoying a brisk game and were approaching the eighth hole, alongside which ran a main road. As the men moved on to the green a funeral procession moved slowly past along the road and one of the foursome removed his cap and stood with his head solemnly bowed as the hearse and accompanying cars passed by.

One of his friends noticed his action and was abashed.

"My gosh, Jim. You remind us all of our manners. It's not often though that one sees such a genuine gesture of respect for the dead."

"Oh, it's the least I could do," replied the man. "You know in six more days we would have been married twenty-five years."

"Caddie, why do you keep looking at your watch?"

"It ain't a watch, sir, it's a compass."

Judge: "Do you understand the nature of an oath?"
Boy: "Do I? I'm your caddie, remember!"

Then there's the one about the golfer and his caddie who enjoyed a good argument, especially about what clubs to use. The caddie usually won but this day, faced with a long short hole, the golfer decided that a 3–iron would be best.

"Take a spoon," growled the caddie.

But the golfer stuck to his choice and the caddie watched gloomily as the ball sailed over the fairway, landed neatly on the green and rolled politely into the hole.

"You see," grinned the triumphant golfer.

"You would have done still better with your spoon," came the dogged reply.

The lady golfer was a determined, if not very proficient player. At each swipe she made at the ball earth flew in all directions.

"Gracious me," she exclaimed red-faced to her caddie, "the worms will think there's an earthquake."

"I don't know," replied the caddie, "the worms round here are very clever. I'll bet most of them are hiding underneath the ball for safety."

Manchester to Melbourne, Perthshire to Palm Springs, the links on a Sunday morning get rather crowded no matter where and veterans throughout the world get irritated by delays.

Mackenzie and Brown were playing their usual weekend match on the links at Royal Sydney and were annoyed by an unusually slow twosome in front of them. One of them was seen to be mooching around on the fairway while the other was searching distractedly in the rough.

"Hey," shouted Brown, "why don't you help your friend find his bloody ball?"

"He's *got* his bloody ball," came the reply. "It's his bloody club he's looking for."

A golfer has one advantage over a fisherman. He doesn't have to produce anything to prove his story.

That he was a wealthy American tourist was obvious. On his arrival at a small Irish hotel the tiny reception area became full in an instant. Not only were there suitcases but also golf clubs, golf shoes, golf umbrellas and several boxes of balls.

"Surely now, sor," cried the manager eyeing the baggage with alarm, "there must be some mistake. We've no golf course you see and you'll be finding there's not one within miles of the place."

"Well now, that's no problem," drawled the tourist. "I'm having one sent over with my heavy baggage."

After a series of disastrous holes, the strictly amateur golfer in an effort to smother his rage laughed hollowly and said to his caddie:

"This golf is a funny game."

"It's not supposed to be," said the boy gravely.

At a Surrey golf club two sedate matrons were playing when a flasher rushed out of the bushes clad in nothing at all.

"Sir," asked the older of the two players severely, "are you a member?"

"My game's really improving, dear."
   "How's that, Mavis?"
   "I hit a ball in one today."

"Your ball hit me!"
   "Not mine, it was my husband's."
   "What are you going to do about it?"
   "Want to hit him back?"

"Bill, I'm giving up, I've swung at that wee ball ten times and missed it every time."
   "Keep trying dear. You've got it looking a bit worried."

"I say greenkeeper, I dropped my bottle of Scotch out of the bag somewhere on the seventh. Anything handed in at lost-and-found?"

"Only the golfer who played after you, sir."

The argumentative drunk in the club bar had been looking for a fight all afternoon since losing his game. Finally he threw a punch at the player on the nearest bar stool. He ducked and the drunk, losing balance, fell off his stool and onto the floor. By the time he'd disentangled himself from bar stools and dusted himself off, his opponent had left.

"D'ya see that, barman?" he complained. "Not much of a fighter was he?"

"Not much of a driver either, sir. He's just driven over your clubs," said the barman gazing out the window.

Explorer: "There we were surrounded. Fierce savages everywhere you looked. They uttered awful cries and beat their clubs on the ground..."

Weary listener: "Golfers, probably."

Paddy and Mick were returning to their native land to play in the All Eire Champions Golf Tournament. Halfway across the Atlantic the pilot of their plane announced over the intercom:

"Ladies and gentlemen. This is your captain speaking. I regret to say that we have lost the use of the outer starboard engine. But there is nothing to worry about. We still have three perfectly good engines which will get us to Shannon airport."

And an hour later the captain's voice was once again heard:

"Ladies and gentlemen. It's the outer port engine that's gone this time. But nothing to worry about, we still have two good engines."

Another half hour passed and once again the captain came on the intercom:

"Ladies and gentlemen. I do regret to announce that the inner starboard engine has gone..."

"Begorrah, Mick," Paddy turned to his mate with a worried expression. "If we lose that fourth engine, we'll not only miss the tee off, we'll be up here all night!"

"I've just killed my wife," cried the hysterical golfer rushing into the clubhouse. "I didn't see her. She was behind me you see," he sobbed, "and I started my back swing and clipped her right between the eyes. She must have died on the instant."

"What club were you using?" asked a concerned bystander.

"Oh, the No. 2 iron."

"Oh, oh," murmured the other, "that's the club that always gets me into trouble too."

Misjudging its depth, Ron went wading into the lake to retrieve his badly sliced ball. Very quickly he was floundering out of his depth and, as his tweed plus-fours became waterlogged, found himself in real trouble.

"Help, I'm drowning!" he shouted to his partner.

"Don't worry," came the reply. "You won't drown. You'll never keep your head down long enough."

The party games were a triumph and now the marble tournament was in full swing. Then six-year-old Simon missed an easy shot and let fly with a potent expletive.

"Simon," his mother remonstrated in embarrassment from the sidelines, "what do little boys who swear when they are playing marbles turn into?"

"Golfers," Simon replied.

Did you hear about the player who spent so much time in the bunker he got mail addressed to Hitler?

Golfer: "Notice any improvement today, Jimmy?"
Caddie: "Yes, ma'am. You've had your hair done."

Somehow it happened that Geoff, the Club's renowned drunk, ended up playing with Sister Mary Xavier from St Francis's Convent.

They were teeing off at the first tee. Sister Mary's drive was clean and straight. Geoff swung at the ball with an uncontrolled lunge. "Dammit," he said, "I missed!"

The good nun frowned but resisted the temptation to lecture.

Geoff took a second swing at the ball but again it was wild. "Dammit, I missed," he cursed.

Sister Mary looked cross but held her tongue.

Geoff's third swing chopped out a goodly quantity of turf but his ball remained immobile.

"Dammit. I missed again!" he shouted.

This was too much for Sister Mary. "Sir," she remonstrated, "if you continue to use such foul language the heavens may open up and the good Lord may smite you with a mighty lightning bolt."

Geoff stood swaying quietly listening to the good nun's message then once again he addressed his ball. Another mighty swing... and again he missed.

"Dammit. I missed!" he cried beating the earth with his club.

At that moment the heavens were rent with a fierce bolt of lightning which flashed down onto the course and hit... Sister Mary.

A mighty voice rang through the universe: "Dammit. I missed!"

A newcomer was to learn the great game at New Zealand's Otago Golf Club.

"And how does one play this game?" he asked his caddie.

The caddie explained about teeing off and the course and his clubs — the irons and woods and so on, but he finished by saying:

"Basically sir, all you have to do is hit the ball in the direction of that flag over there."

"Right ho," and the novice teed off. It was a magnificent drive that took his ball right down the centre of the fairway. And, unbelievably, it landed on the green only a few centimetres from the hole.

"What do I do now?" asked the novice.

"Just hit the ball into the hole sir," said the caddie in some excitement. "That's the whole idea of the game."

"*Now* you tell me!"

"**I** say, what happened to you, Carruthers?" enquired the secretary of the Berkhampstead Country Club.

The player whom he addressed was sitting staring morosely ahead, a neat whisky in one hand and his bandaged head in the other.

"Damned extraordinary business. Hooked me drive on the eleventh. Ball landed in the cow pasture beside the fairway. Couldn't find the damned thing."

"How very annoying. But what happened then? Did the cow have a go at you?"

"No, no. Was standin' there wonderin' when a memsahib playing behind me led off. Hooked her ball too... same direction as mine. So, thought... find her ball, find mine. D'y'see?"

"Do go on, old man."

"Lookin', y'see, and one of those damned cows walked past and swished up its tail... and there was a golf ball stuck firmly in place. Too far away though to know if my ball or the mem's."

"Yes?"

"Just then the mem jumped over the fence and asked 'Have you seen a golf ball?' 'Course I walked over to the cow, lifted its tail and enquired, 'Look like yours?' *That's* what happened to me!"

Eric, the club's worst golfer, was addressing his ball. Feet apart, just so, eye on the ball, just so, a few practice wiffles with the driver, just so, then swing. He missed. The procedure was repeated and then repeated again. On the fourth swing however he did manage to connect with his ball and drove it five metres down the fairway. Looking up in exasperation he saw a stranger who had stopped to watch him.

"Look here!" Eric shouted angrily. "Only golfers are allowed on this course!"

The stranger nodded, "I know it, mister," he replied. "But I won't say anything if you won't either!"

The old golfer paced anxiously up and down outside the emergency room of the East Lothian Hospital near Muirfield Golf Course. Inside the doctors were operating to remove a golf ball accidentally driven down a player's throat.

The sister-in-charge noticed the old golfer and went to reassure him.

"It won't be long now," she said. "You're a relative?"

"No, no, lassie. It's my ball."

Talk about fantastic golf teachers. He was the best and one day this woman came to him and said that she had developed a terrific slice.

Day and night he worked with her for five months. Now she's the biggest hooker in town.

At the Glenelg seaside course in South Australia a novice managed a mighty drive off the first tee. It hit, and bounced off in rapid succession, a rock outcrop, a fisherman, a tree trunk, the handle of a golf cart, a player on the second tee and finally it dropped onto the green about ten centimetres from the hole.

"Well," the player exclaimed, "if only I'd hit the bloody ball a bit harder!"

Bob and Ken had been friends for over twenty years and had played golf for over twenty years and, what is more, for over twenty years, Bob had lost each game. Well, that can only go on for so long — finally the worm has to turn and things have to change. Bob decided to get the greatest partner to help him beat the unbeatable Ken. So he found this giant Irish wharf labourer and got him on side.

They were out on the first tee with the hole some 400 metres off and the giant hit a tremendous drive which landed the ball on the green.

"I can't beat that," Ken moaned. "He'll probably go two on every hole. Here's the money. Incidentally, though, how does he putt?"

Bob carefully pocketed his win. "Same way he drives," he replied.

He was not what you'd call an expert player. Time after time he would hit his brand new balls where they couldn't be retrieved or even found. Balls went into the lake, out of bounds, across the highway, into the woods, and on one memorable occasion into a stormwater drain that was being built near the course.

It was after that shot that one of the members of his foursome suggested, "Why don't you use an old ball on those difficult shots?"

"An old ball?" the benighted player cried. "The way I play, surely it's obvious I've never had an old ball!"

His wife was a new and nervous player but Jim persuaded her to play against a new customer of his and his wife.

"After all," he explained, "it will be a two-ball foursome. I'll drive off and by the time you have to hit the ball the client and his spouse will be elsewhere on the fairway and not watching you."

It was agreed and the game started as Jim had said it would. He hit off with a fine drive, right down the fairway about 320 metres leaving about four metres to the green. He handed his wife an iron and told her to aim for the green. She sliced it with vigour into the deep rough at the side of the fairway. Two! His shot from the rough was magnificent and landed the ball back on the fairway — this time about half a metre from the green. Three! She whacked it right over the green and into the sandtrap on the other side. Four! He was in brilliant form and he clipped it neatly from the sand onto the green about a metre from the hole. Five! Her putt rolled off the green and into another sandtrap. Six! His recovery landed three centimetres from the hole. Seven! Her putt stopped at the green's edge. Eight! His putt of thirteen metres went in. Nine!

The customer and his wife holed out with four.

Jim's reaction was nothing too dramatic. He merely tore up his score card and ate it, broke three clubs and bent the remainder, jumped up and down on his golfcart and finally, shaking his fist at his wife, he strode off to the clubhouse.

His wife emerged from the sandtrap whence she had watched the performance. "I don't know what he's so mad about," she said. "After all, he had five; I only had four!"

An Australian touring round Britain was playing on a small course in Devonshire. He was on the first green and about to putt when he was suddenly beset by a flock of seagulls.

"Piss off, will ya'," he cried, thrashing at the birds.

A sweet little old lady who was sitting knitting near the green came over to speak to him.

"Excuse me," she said. "There's no need to speak to the little birdies like that. All you need to say is 'Shoo shoo little birdies!' Then they'll piss off."

"Let me inform you, young man," said the slow elderly golfer, "I was playing this game before you were born."

"That's all very well, but I'd be obliged if you'd try to finish it before I die."

Then there was the day the course was invaded by another al fresco diner.

An old tramp had wandered leisurely up to the green of the eighteenth where he sat himself down among his many coats. He dug among the variety of old bags he was carrying and brought forth with great pomp a handful of dried twigs and two iron rods which he arranged to form into a holder. From this he hung a pot of water suspended over the twigs.

Members gathering at the clubhouse windows watched as he got his campfire going. The tranquillity of the scene was shattered when a man dashed from the clubhouse and, leaving no room for doubt, ordered the tramp off the course.

"Well, just who do you think you are," asked the tramp.

"I'm the club secretary," shouted the man.

"Well, listen sonny," the tramp retorted. "Let me give you some advice. That's hardly the way to get new members."

As the two players approached the ninth tee they noticed what appeared to be a small picnic party assembled right on the spot.

"Here, what are you doing with our tee?" one called out.

"Garn, it ain't yours," came the retort. "We brought it wiv us all the way from Bermondsey."

Hempenshaw was playing off the sixth tee at the Royal Quebec Club. The fairway of the sixth needed some skill because it ran alongside the road. But Hempenshaw sliced the ball badly and it disappeared over the hedge bordering the road. So he put another ball down and took the penalty.

He was having a beer after the game when the pro joined him in the bar.

"Excuse me M. Hempenshaw, but was it you who sliced this ball into the road at the sixth this morning?"

"Yes, but I took the penalty."

"That's as may be, monsieur. But you might be interested to know that your ball hit and killed a small boy on a tricycle; the tricycle fell in the path of a mountie on a motorcycle. He skidded and was thrown through the window of a car, killing the nun at the wheel. The car then swerved into a cement mixer which wasn't too damaged but had to veer slightly and in doing so ran into the local school bus with such an impact that it sent it flying through the window of the St Lawrence shopping centre. At last count from the hospital there are thirteen people dead and seventy-nine people seriously injured."

The golfer turned a deathly shade of white and said, "What can I do?"

"Well, you *could* try moving your left hand a little bit further down the shaft," the pro advised.

Moishe and Abraham decided to join the best golf club that money could buy. On their first day they went into the bar for a drink before the game. They ordered two whiskies and enquired:

"How much is that?"

The barman smiled. "Are you new members?" he asked. "This your first day at the club?"

"Yes," replied Moishe and Abraham.

"Well, it's on the house."

Then the two friends decided to lunch in the club dining room. It was a sumptuous repast after which Abraham called the waitress over.

"We'd like to settle up," he said.

The waitress smiled sweetly and enquired whether they were new members.

"Yes," they told her, "we are indeed."

"And is this your first day at the club?"

"Yes," they replied.

"Then, it's on the house, sirs."

Much pleased, the two decided it was time to have a game so they walked into the pro shop to buy some balls.

"Give me half a dozen," Moishe ordered grandly. "How much is that?"

"Are you new members, sir? Is it your first day at the club?"

"Yes, yes," smiled Moishe.

"That will be seventy-five dollars," the pro advised.

Moishe turned to Abraham and whispered:

"It sure ain't by the throat they got you in this club."

Sam and Janet were beginning a game of golf. Janet stepped to the tee, and her first drive gave her a hole in one. Sam stepped up to the tee and said, "OK, now I'll take my practice swing, and then we'll start the game."

He had just come in from a long afternoon at golf. His wife kissed him and kissed their son who came in a few seconds later.

"Where's he been?" the husband asked.

"He's been caddying for you all afternoon," the wife replied.

"No wonder that kid looked so familiar!"

"Really, I can't play golf," said the blonde. "I don't even know how to hold the caddie."

Two long-time enthusiasts were discussing their scores over a beer in the clubhouse.

"I can't understand it one cried disgustedly. "I've been playing golf for fifteen years now and I get worse every year. Do you know, last year I played worse than the year before. And the year before that, same thing.

"That's depressing," commiserated the other. "How're you doing this year?"

"Put it this way," said the first, nursing his beer unhappily. "I am already playing next year's game."

Mark Twain accompanied a friend and watched while the friend played golf. Repeatedly during the game more turf was hit than golf balls and dirt went flying after every stroke.

Finally the friend turned to Twain and enquired how he liked the links.

"Best I ever tasted," came the swift reply.

Which possibly led Twain to the following conclusion:
Golf is a good walk spoiled.